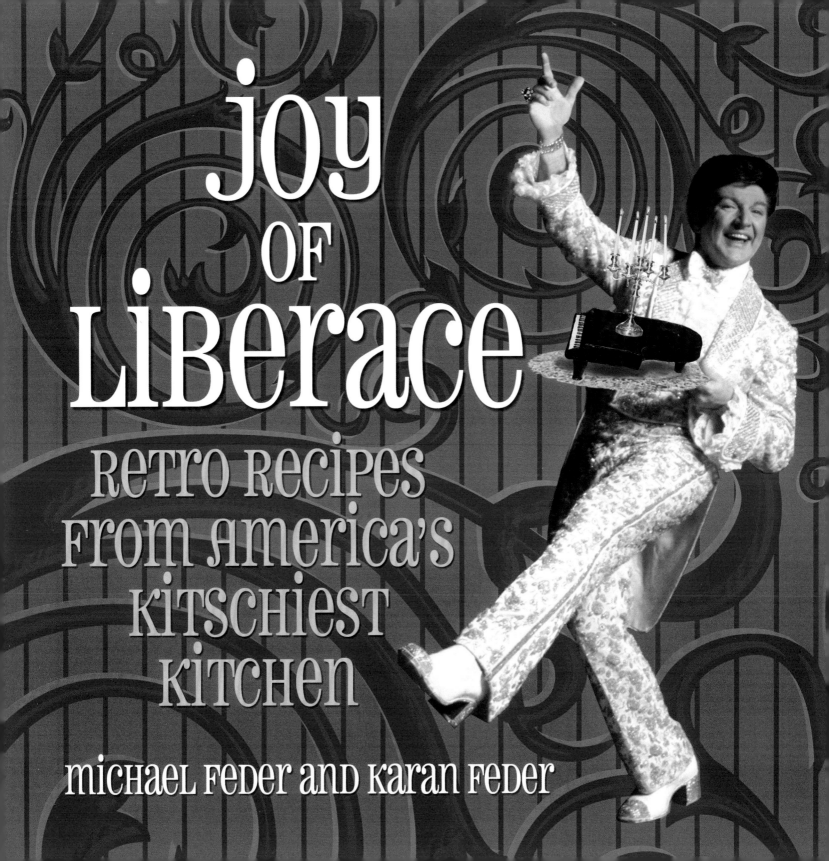

joy
OF
Liberace

Retro Recipes From America's Kitschiest Kitchen

michael feder and karan feder

Joy of Liberace: Retro Recipes from America's Kitschiest Kitchen
Copyright © 2007 by Michael Feder and Karan Feder

Designed by Amy Inouye, www.futurestudio.com

First edition
10 9 8 7 6 5 4 3 2 1

ISBN-13 978-1-883318-71-0 / ISBN-10 1-883318-71-8

Library of Congress Cataloging-in-Publication Data

Feder, Michael (W. Michael)
 Joy of Liberace : retro recipes from America's kitschiest kitchen /
by Michael Feder and Karan Feder.
    p. cm.
ISBN 978-1-883318-71-0 (paperbound : alk. paper)
1. Cookery. 2. Liberace, 1919-1987. I. Feder, Karan. II. Title.
TX714.F437 2007
 641.5–dc22

               2007007948

Printed in Canada

ACP

ANGEL CITY PRESS

2118 Wilshire Blvd. #880
Santa Monica, California 90403
310.395.9982
www.angelcitypress.com

Citizens' National Trust and Savings Bank was
The Liberace Show's first advertising sponsor.
The first fifteen-minute episode of this prime time
television series aired on NBC in 1952.

CONTENTS

acknowledgments

The authors gratefully acknowledge the support of the Liberace Foundation and its Board of Directors.

We'd also like to express our appreciation to the hardworking staff and volunteers at the Liberace Museum, without whom there would be no Liberace legacy preserved for all of us to enjoy.

Very Special Thanks go to John Neeland, our friend and Riviera Hotel public relations wizard who paved the way and made it possible to work with Liberace's favorite hotel. We are also grateful to Rick Baumes, assistant executive chef who has been with the Riviera for twenty-four years. We are also grateful to Sam Chong, executive chef who has spent five years at the Riviera; Cindy Ellis, *garde manger* chef in her first year at the hotel; Paul Martinez, assistant pastry chef who has worked for the Riviera for more than eighteen years; Tom Martinez, the amazing executive pastry chef who has spent four decades at the hotel, and everyone else at the Riviera who helped make our historic collaboration a success.

We'd also like to express our appreciation to the team at Barrett Photography who did an outstanding job photographing the Riviera's creations, to Madeleine Franco, kind and talented friend, for her help smoothing over some of our awkward sentences, and to Darin Hollingsworth, executive director of the Liberace Foundation, whose suggestions were thought provoking and helped to improve the book.

Finally, thank you to our publishers, Paddy Calistro and Scott McAuley, for their unwavering faith in this project from beginning to end, and to the uncommonly talented folks at Angel City Press, especially graphic designer Amy Inouye, without whom this culinary compendium would not be what it is today.

Liberace tips his hat in thanks to the Riviera for his birthday gifts—a fancy cake complete with candelabrum and that shiny red Mercedes convertible underneath the cake.

Liberace [lib•r•AH•chee], 1) n., Wladziu Valentino Liberace (b. May 16, 1919, d. February 4, 1987), known by stage name Liberace and Mr. Showmanship (or, to friends, Lee), the single most charismatic and flamboyant American entertainer of his time; (2) adj., characterized by the ability to exude flamboyance almost on par with the entertainer (see above), as in "You are So Liberace," (3) n., exuberant consumption, as in "On giant occasions like this, only absolute Liberace will do"

Liberace the performer

Never underestimate a man in a sequined apron. Take Liberace, for instance, who not only had sequined aprons, but bejeweled shoes, neckties, capes and more. At the height of his career he was the world's highest-paid classical pianist, had two stars on Hollywood's Walk of Fame, six Gold Records, two Emmys, and, in the 1950s, his eponymous television show was carried on more stations than *I Love Lucy*. Yet his standing-room-only crowds for his shows in Las Vegas—and at the most prestigious hotels and venues in the largest cities in the nation—were only part of his success.

In fact, Liberace was truly a showman, in every sense of the word, and his fans loved his mutiny against moderation. His diamonds, feathers and glitter were the Bling that brightened mid-century America. Who else could pull-off white damask tails with rhinestoned lapels one day and red-white-and-blue sequined hot pants the next? Or a pinkie ring diamond that weighed down his hand? His unfettered visual exuberance earned him a coveted place on *People* magazine's Best-Dressed List, and that said a lot, because extravagant indulgence wasn't everybody's style—but it was So Liberace.

Liberace happily fell on the sword of shameless excess and, in so doing, made poking fun at himself a hapless endeavor for anyone else—he was way too good at it. Liberace was in on the joke and laughing all the way to the bank—or to the buffet table. You see, the guy not only could play like a maestro, bedazzle an audience and dress like a diva, Liberace could cook.

This multi-talented life began May 16, 1919 in West Allis, Wisconsin. Young Wladziu Liberace was classically trained as a pianist and became somewhat of a child prodigy, winning an early piano scholarship, and performing as a soloist with the Chicago Symphony at age fourteen. His older brother George was an accomplished violinist, and gave the gifted young Wladziu his first opportunities as a professional. After changing his stage name to simply Liberace, the pianist's classical career expanded. In time he realized that witty encores, during which he played snippets of pop songs and marches, went over better with audiences than did his main-program classical pieces. Shifting his act to what he called "classical music with the boring parts left out," and ultimately "pop with a bit of classics," Liberace fully developed his musical trademark of

Liberace cooks in his musical kitchen.

technical proficiency with passionately flamboyant flourishes.

He was discovered by Hollywood when he played at the Hotel del Coronado in San Diego and soon found himself an overnight success, headlining in a summer replacement for television's *Dinah Shore Show.* By 1952 Liberace was the star of his own network program—a musical variety show that included his brother George as the bandleader. Soon Liberace's show was scoring higher ratings than *I Love Lucy.* Through his TV show and personal appearances, Liberace fast became known for his extravagant costumes, personal charm and self-deprecating wit. He also established his most famous personal trademark, a silver candelabrum set on his piano, candles flaming.

Liberace sold more than two million records in 1953, and, by 1955, the same year he starred in the film *Sincerely Yours* with Dorothy Malone, he was making fifty thousand dollars a week performing at the famed Riviera Hotel in Las Vegas.

Beginning the decade of the Sixties with a bang, Liberace performed at the London Palladium with Nat King Cole and Sammy Davis, Jr., in a groundbreaking live musical telecast attended by Queen Elizabeth II. He starred in the 1965 movie *When the Boys Meet the Girls* co-starring Connie Francis, and followed that the next year with a role as a casket salesman in *The Loved One*, his only non-piano playing gig, for which he garnered excellent reviews. Liberace also appeared in two top-rated episodes of the television series *Batman*, going on to guest-

Liberace was America's first television idol.

star in *Here's Lucy, Kojak, The Muppet Show, Saturday Night Live, The Tonight Show* and the 1985 World Wrestling Foundation's feature, *Wrestlemania.*

Throughout the 1970s and 1980s Liberace played to packed houses in Las Vegas and elsewhere, pulling down paychecks of three hundred thousand dollars a week.

As a tribute to himself and to the dazzling lifestyle that had become synonymous with his name, Liberace opened the Liberace Museum in Las Vegas in 1979. The museum showcases many of his stage costumes, cars, jewelry and furniture pieces, including his collection of historic and lavishly decorated pianos. Within the walls of this monument to excess, Liberace's treasures have become the Bling paradigm, the benchmarks for all things considered "Totally Liberace."

Liberace's final stage performance was at Radio City Music Hall in New York City on November 2, 1986, and his last public appearance was on *Oprah!* the day after Christmas. Liberace died February 4, 1987 in Palm Springs, California. Liberace is interred at the Forest Lawn Memorial Park in California, right next to his beloved mother and brother. The Liberace Museum continues to welcome visitors from around the world.

He will be forever Mr. Showmanship, and we know that Liberace continues to whip up heavenly dishes for all those near and dear, most certainly bringing the spirit of his music and his candelabrum to entertain and amuse appreciative souls in the very highest of places.

Liberace the Chef

In addition to caring for his beloved dogs, Liberace's favorite hobbies were shopping for antiques, interior decorating, collecting miniature pianos and cooking. While he was passionate about all of those pursuits, Liberace truly adored cooking. Food and its preparation stirred warm memories that reached far back into Liberace's early childhood.

Throughout his lifetime, Liberace maintained a legendary intimacy with his mother, Frances. When his parents divorced during the very early stages of his career, Liberace remained close only to his mother, who moved in with him. Frances, in addition to preparing all the family meals, had worked in a cookie factory when Liberace was a child. Liberace's warm memories of fresh cookies and the smell of baking, together with his beloved mother's cookie experience, inspired the original Liberace recipe for the seriously delectable Fabulous Florentines found in the Razzle Dazzle Decadence chapter that's filled with Liberace's favorite desserts.

So it seems that Liberace's passion for cooking was as genetic as his gift for music. In high school, Liberace pioneered a chef's course which, he modestly recalled, "became very popular with my fellow students." The fascination with food continued. In his adult years, Liberace often prepared meals for friends and associates and, of course, for his family. He cooked for his mother, using many of her own recipes in his culinary repertoire. In fact, cooking was so important to him that, while on the road, he reported that "I carried my own utensils—pots, pans, and dishes—all the [hotel] had to supply was a refrigerator and an electric stove, which were placed on a temporary platform over the bathtub." (This would break all kinds of fire laws today, not to mention setting off the hotel sprinkler system, so please don't try this yourself. After all, Liberace was a master chef).

One of the many friends Liberace cooked for in his hotel room-"kitchen" was Mike Douglas, of talk-show-host fame. Liberace, of course, preferred his home kitchen, where he entertained many celebrities over the years, to great success, except the most famous one—Michael Jackson. Liberace surprised the King of Pop with "a real Southern soul-food meal," which included fried chicken. Liberace reported that "on the way into the dining room, Michael said, 'Oh, I forgot to tell you—I'm a vegetarian.'" By his own admission, vegetarian meals were definitely "not Liberace."

Liberace owned a popular Italian restaurant in Las Vegas, Tivoli Gardens (named after the famous Copenhagen amusement park with its diverse collection of restaurants, a place Liberace called "unforgettable"). Not satisfied with being a passive investor in the establishment, Liberace was a very active participant—so much so that he had an apartment built in the back of the eatery so he could tweak the sauces at just a moment's notice. Location, location, location!

Themed rooms such as the English Room, Swan Room, Antique Room and Orchid Room (for Liberace's mother, who had an orchid named after her), were encircled with twinkling lights, crystals and mirrors with Liberace's theme song "I'll Be Seeing You" engraved into them. It was all set off by what was, at the time, the world's largest piano bar. The place was most assuredly a Liberace production, and well worthy of the accolade, "Totally Liberace!"

The restaurant accommodated as many as three hundred patrons at a time, including top stars such as Dolly Parton and Frank Sinatra, who were lavished with the same glamorous royal treatment that Liberace enjoyed in his own private life. The coup de grâce was when Liberace entertained King Carl XVI Gustaf of Sweden at Tivoli Gardens, and Mr. Showmanship's royal talent became official—media coverage proclaimed "The food was indeed fit for a King."

Many of the recipes in this book were featured at the restaurant, which is now called Carluccio's Tivoli Gardens. Still in its original location in the Liberace Museum plaza, the restaurant is a popular Liberace gem and Las Vegas landmark, with its original wooden doors decorated with hand-carved L's, and much of its interior meticulously preserved.

When it came to entertaining at home, Liberace's style was an extension of his stage act, filled to capacity with Bling, glitz and glam. Even as he was laughing all the way to the bank professionally, he was laughing all the way to the buffet table privately. Liberace loved to delight his guests with his own recipes and his uniquely spectacular style of presentation. Liberace's almost infinite cash flow allowed him to entertain in whatever manner he so desired. And he so desired pretty much everything, everywhere, all the time. Liberace's exuberant stamp was on every area of his life, and left no corner, baseboard, curtain or bathroom untouched. He was a man who demanded the finest, and had the wherewithal to pay for it. Witness: Liberace's glassware and goblets were specially made for him by the royal glassmaker to Queen Elizabeth II, who recreated her private pattern especially for him.

Liberace and the Riviera Hotel in Las Vegas

The relationship between Liberace and the Riviera Hotel dates to the mid-Fifties. At the time the newest hotel and casino in Las Vegas, the Riviera was called a "high-rise hotel," ascending, as it did, to the commanding height of nine stories. For such a lofty affair, the Riviera naturally looked for an entertainer with stratospheric popularity. Liberace was unanimously chosen to be the "featured performer" for the Riviera's grand-opening celebration in April of 1955, and he cut the opening day ribbon. He was paid the record-breaking sum of fifty thousand dollars per week for the gig and then continued performing at the Riviera for another twenty-eight years.

Liberace was so sizzling hot in 1956—the biggest star in the entertainment universe—that he was asked to introduce a new talent, Elvis Presley. As Liberace recalled, "Elvis was a teenage sensation, but the people in Vegas didn't know what to make of him. He lacked the showmanship, production, costumes . . . so Elvis's manager, Colonel Parker, came to see me. He said 'My boy is appearing across the street. He's havin' some problems . . . He admires you so much. If I could bring him over for a picture, he'd really appreciate it.' Elvis came. We switched jackets. I held his guitar, while he sat at the piano . . . One thing about Elvis—he never forgot a friend. Every opening night, I got a guitar made of fresh flowers." And eventually, as Elvis's career matured, the world saw Colonel Parker's boy become a bit Liberace himself, right down to the sequins, rhinestones and capes.

The Royal Court—Liberace and Elvis Presley
exchange jackets and instruments.

Ribbon-cutting at the Riviera, 1955.

How fitting, then, that two original Las Vegas
legends—Liberace and the Riviera—are united again in *Joy
of Liberace*. Dishes from this collection of retro recipes
from Liberace's kitchen are masterfully interpreted and
executed by the culinary staff of the Riviera Hotel and
Casino in the Liberace tradition of flamboyance, flash
and fluff.

Like Liberace, the Riviera's superb culinary staff
has its own grand and storied history:

Cm7   E♭/F   F7   Fm6   G9   G7♭9

"Too much of a good thing is won . . . der . . . ful!"

in   ev -'ry - thing   that's light   and   gay,   I'll   al - ways   think of you   that way.   I'll

Fun Riviera Culinary Facts:

Executive Head Pastry Chef Tom Martinez is the longest-serving pastry chef on the Strip, with four decades at the Riviera. Not only did Chef Martinez see Liberace perform at the Riviera, he personally made pastry for Liberace when the entertainer had a hankering for something sweet—which was often.

The Riviera's executive culinary staff, who helped realize Liberace's Bling Cooking, has, collectively, more than one hundred years of culinary experience, with most of that experience at the Riviera. The Riviera employs approximately two hundred fifty people in its nine kitchens (serving six retail restaurants and a food court) and banquet kitchens that serve approximately one million meals per year, twenty-four hours a day, seven days a week. From private room service to giant conventions, the Riviera culinary staff is on par with the very finest in the world.

The Riviera team's creations for *Joy of Liberace* are as over-the-top as the piano talent who provided the inspiration. Filled with rich flavor and decorated with sparkly Bling—these dishes are the very essence of Bling Cooking. The Rivera masters helped invent an exciting new tradition: the Liberace Bling Cake party.

Henceforth, every February, starting on the 1st and leading up to the anniversary of Liberace's death on the 4th, go totally Liberace and plan your own Bling Cake Party, inviting all your fabulous friends. Make sure to finish the evening by serving slices of Liberace's Exceptional and Extraordinary Angel Bling Cake Pie (the recipe is in Chapter 5, Razzle Dazzle Decadence). Don't forget to bake in a Bling trinket! He who is served the hidden Bling is bestowed the supreme honor of hosting the next night's Liberace Bling Cake soiree.

Tom Martinez, executive head pastry chef; Paul Martinez, assistant pastry chef; Sam Chong, executive chef; Cindy Ellis, *garde manger* chef; and Rick Baumes, assistant executive chef.

Bada Bing, Bada Bling

Liberace means "the more the merrier" in Italian—at least when it comes to house guests

While it is true that Liberace's instrument of distinction was exuberant excess, he was in on the joke and laughed right along with his audiences. When it came to his beloved guests, nothing was too much. One never worried about running out of food while dining at the Liberace house.

Here you will find recipes that you can scale up to serve as many fans as possible—Carpe Diem Curried Scrambled Eggs could just as well serve 4 or 400, and Liberace's pasta dishes are designed to fill you up until you wonder if he had an elastic waistband in those bejeweled trousers he wore.

Liberace serves a spaghetti dinner to his co-workers, the Merial Dancers at the Palmer House in Chicago.

carpe diem curried scrambled eggs

8 eggs

8 teaspoons water or milk

½ teaspoon salt

⅛ teaspoon pepper

2 tablespoons butter

1 teaspoon curry

Serves 3 to 4

Crack the eggs into a bowl.

Add water or milk if desired.

Add salt and pepper, mix with a fork or whisk.

Melt butter in pan over low heat and cook eggs gently. Stir the eggs as they cook; a wooden spoon works well for this.

Add 1 teaspoon curry.

When eggs are not quite firm, remove from heat. The eggs will continue to cook while in the hot pan.

Liberace hails a cab in style!

italian tomato salad

2 small onions, thinly sliced
    into rings
8 tomatoes, peeled and
    cut into segments
1 teaspoon salt
½ teaspoon pepper
½ teaspoon sugar
1 teaspoon thyme leaves or
    ½ teaspoon powdered thyme
2 tablespoons olive oil

Serves 8

Separate the onion rings and mix with the tomatoes in a salad bowl.

Add the salt, pepper, sugar and thyme.

Pour the olive oil over and refrigerate for at least an hour.

italian bread with cheese

1 large loaf Italian Bread
¼ cup soft butter
1 five-ounce jar Cheddar cheese
    spread
½ teaspoon prepared mustard
2 tablespoons sherry

Serves 6 to 8

Preheat broiler.

Cut the bread lengthwise, then make diagonal slits without cutting all the way through.

Blend the butter and cheese with the mustard and sherry and place in the slits, spreading a little on top of the bread.

Heat under the broiler, cut-side up.

1½ dozen cherrystone or

    littleneck clams or

    2 eight-ounce cans, minced

1 garlic clove, minced

¼ cup olive oil

1 one-pound, four-ounce can

    Italian plum tomatoes,

    drained

2 tablespoons minced parsley

½ teaspoon salt

1 pound spaghettini

Serves 4 to 6

If you can get fresh clams, scrub and open them, reserving juice. Chop the clams.

Brown the garlic in 3 tablespoons oil.

Add reserved clam juice, clams, tomatoes and parsley.

Simmer for ½ hour.

Add salt and simmer 3 more minutes.

Meanwhile, cook the spaghettini in a large pot of boiling salted water with remaining 1 tablespoon olive oil for 12 minutes. Drain.

Pour the sauce over the steaming drained spaghettini.

Baked Stuffed Mostaccioli

2 pounds mostaccioli

¾ pound lean beef,
    ground twice

¼ pound ground lean pork

¼ pound grated Parmesan
    cheese

1 garlic clove, minced

2 tablespoons minced parsley

½ cup breadcrumbs

1 teaspoon salt

¼ teaspoon freshly ground
    pepper

grating of nutmeg, to taste

3 eggs, slightly beaten

tomato sauce

grated Parmesan or
    Romano cheese

Serves 8 to 10

Preheat oven to 350 degrees (F).

Butter a 9 × 13-inch baking dish.

Parboil the mostaccioli until pliable, drain and cool.

Mix meats with Parmesan, garlic, parsley and breadcrumbs.

Season with salt, pepper and nutmeg.

Add eggs to mixture.

Use a pastry tube to fill mostaccioli. If mixture is not soft enough to squeeze through the opening, add a little of the tomato sauce or some broth.

Put a layer of pasta into prepared dish, cover with tomato sauce and sprinkle with cheese.

Repeat layering, ending with sauce and cheese.

Bake for 1 hour.

Liberace shows off his Rolls-Royce and his poodle, Baby Boy, in front of his Palm Springs home. The first car Liberace owned was an Oldsmobile 88. A fitting choice for Liberace since there are 88 keys on the piano.

italian pork chops

0 loin pork chops, 1 inch thick

2 teaspoons salt

½ teaspoon pepper

3 tablespoons flour

2 tablespoons olive oil

2 tablespoons butter

½ cup chopped onion

¼ cup chopped celery

1 one-pound, four-ounce can

   Italian tomatoes

1 six-ounce can tomato paste

1 teaspoon sugar

¼ teaspoon oregano

¼ teaspoon thyme

1 garlic clove, crushed

½ cup dry red wine

¼ cup grated Parmesan cheese

Serves 8

Sprinkle the chops with salt and pepper and dust with flour.

Heat oil with butter in a skillet or casserole and brown chops on both sides. Remove chops and set aside.

Brown the onion and celery in the same pan for 2 or 3 minutes.

Add tomatoes, tomato paste, sugar, oregano, thyme and garlic.

Add the pork chops and simmer, covered, for 15 minutes.

Add the wine and simmer 15 minutes more.

Sprinkle the Parmesan cheese over before serving.

2 pounds small zucchini

1 large onion (or 4 scallions),
    minced

2 tablespoons butter

2 tomatoes, peeled and chopped,
    or 1 cup canned tomatoes,
    drained

1 teaspoon sugar

1 teaspoon salt

¼ teaspoon pepper

¼ to ½ teaspoon oregano or basil

½ pound small fresh mushrooms,
    cleaned

Serves 6

Do not peel the zucchini.

Slice in rounds and simmer in salted water for 7 minutes. Drain.

Heat butter and brown the onions or scallions 3 minutes.

Add the tomatoes, sugar, salt, pepper and oregano or basil.

Simmer for about 5 minutes and add the zucchini and mushrooms.

Heat for 5 minutes.

swiss twist mac and cheese

4 quarts water

1 tablespoon olive oil

1 tablespoon salt

½ pound Swiss cheese,

    cut into julienne strips

½ pound mozzarella cheese,

    cut into julienne strips

1 pound elbow or other macaroni

½ cup grated Parmesan cheese

3 tablespoons melted butter

Serves 6 to 8

In a large pot, add water with oil and salt. Bring water to a boil and add the macaroni slowly so water will not cool.

If using regular macaroni, break into pieces 2 to 3 inches long.

Cook for 15 minutes.

Meanwhile, melt cheese strips slowly in a small pan over very low heat or in microwave.

Drain macaroni, rinse with hot water and drain again.

Heat broiler.

Butter a baking dish and combine the macaroni with melted cheeses. Stir in half the Parmesan cheese.

Distribute the remaining cheese and melted butter evenly over top.

Place baking dish on low shelf under broiler and heat just until hot and brown on top.

LIBERACE CLASSIC MACARONI AND CHEESE

8 ounces elbow macaroni

2 tablespoons butter

2 tablespoons flour

1½ cups milk

2 cups grated sharp Cheddar cheese

3 tablespoons grated Parmesan cheese

1 teaspoon salt

1 teaspoon grated onion

½ teaspoon monosodium glutamate (optional)

¼ teaspoon dry mustard

dash of cayenne pepper

½ garlic clove, crushed

½ cup coarsely crushed potato chips

paprika

Serves 6

Preheat oven to 350 degrees (F).

Grease a 2-quart casserole.

Cook the macaroni according to package instructions. Drain.

Melt the butter in the top of a double boiler over simmering water, blend in the flour, and gradually stir in the milk. Cook and stir until thickened and smooth.

Add the cheeses and continue to cook and stir until melted.

Add remaining ingredients except potato chips and paprika.

Mix well and add the drained macaroni.

Pour into prepared casserole, sprinkle top with potato chips and dust with paprika.

Bake 20 to 30 minutes until hot and bubbly.

Liberace traveled with his own personal kitchen and cooking supplies in specially fitted Halliburton luggage cases.

iTalian Peas Please

¼ cup olive oil

3 pounds of fresh peas or

    2 boxes frozen

1 tablespoon minced parsley

1 garlic clove, crushed

¼ cup diced ham

½ teaspoon salt

½ teaspoon sugar

½ cup water

Serves 6

Combine all the ingredients in a large pot and bring to a boil.

Cover and simmer for 5 minutes or until peas are tender.

If you are using frozen peas, make certain not to overcook them.

stracciatella

4 eggs

¼ cup grated Parmesan cheese

2 tablespoons fine semolina

6 cups chicken broth

Serves 8

Beat the eggs slightly, add the Parmesan cheese and semolina and mix well.

Heat 2 cups of chicken broth, add egg mixture and heat. Stir until smooth.

Heat the remaining broth and pour in the egg mixture; heat for several minutes and bring almost to a boil.

Serve at once.

chicken cacciatore

2 2½-to 3-pound frying

    chickens, cut up

1 tablespoon salt

¼ teaspoon pepper

flour

¼ cup olive oil

1 large onion, chopped

¼ cup chopped celery

¼ cup chopped parsley

1 pimiento, chopped

1 garlic clove, crushed

1 bay leaf

¼ cup water

½ cup dry white wine

1 cup peeled and diced or

    canned tomatoes, drained

¼ teaspoon sugar

½ teaspoon oregano

¼ pound mushrooms, sliced

Season the chickens with salt and pepper and dredge with a little flour.

Heat oil and lightly brown the onion, celery, parsley, pimiento and garlic.

Add the chicken and bay leaf. Cook until the chicken is light golden.

Add ¼ cup of water and the wine, tomatoes, sugar and oregano.

Cover and simmer for 20 minutes.

Stir in the mushrooms and simmer another 15 minutes.

Liberace holds court at Bimbo's 365 Club in San Francisco.

gilding-the-lily Lasagna

¼ cup olive oil

2 garlic cloves, minced

¼ cup minced celery

1 one-pound, four-ounce can of

    Italian plum tomatoes

½ cup tomato paste

½ cup hot water

½ teaspoon salt

¼ teaspoon pepper

1 pound Italian sausage

1½ pounds lasagna noodles

1½ cups grated Parmesan cheese

1 pound ricotta cheese, crumbled

¾ pound mozzarella cheese,

    cut up

Serves 8

Heat olive oil and sauté the garlic and celery 2 to 3 minutes.

Add the tomatoes and the tomato paste, which has been mixed with the hot water.

Add salt and pepper.

Stir and simmer, covered, for about an hour.

Broil the sausage or sauté it and cut into small pieces.

Cook the noodles in boiling salted water for 12 minutes and drain.

Preheat oven to 350 degrees (F).

To assemble lasagna, pour ½ cup sauce into a 3-quart greased casserole or baking pan.

Put in a layer of noodles, a layer of Parmesan cheese, then noodles, a layer of cut-up mozzarella, a layer of sauce, then ricotta cheese.

Scatter spoonfuls of sausage throughout and continue to layer all the ingredients, topping with sauce and grated Parmesan cheese.

Bake 15 minutes or until thoroughly heated though.

Right Royal Fettucine

¼ pound prosciutto, sliced
into thin strips

½ pound mushrooms, sliced

¼ cup butter

1 pound fettuccini

2 chicken bouillon cubes

2 teaspoons salt

¼ cup grated Parmesan cheese

3 tablespoons heavy cream

Cut the fat from the prosciutto.

Heat 2 tablespoons butter in large pan and sauté prosciutto with mushrooms for 2 to 3 minutes.

Meanwhile, cook the fettuccini in boiling water with bouillon cubes and salt for 8 minutes. Drain.

Put the fettuccini in the pan with mushrooms and ham.

Add the remaining butter, cheese and cream, heat and toss for 2 to 3 minutes.

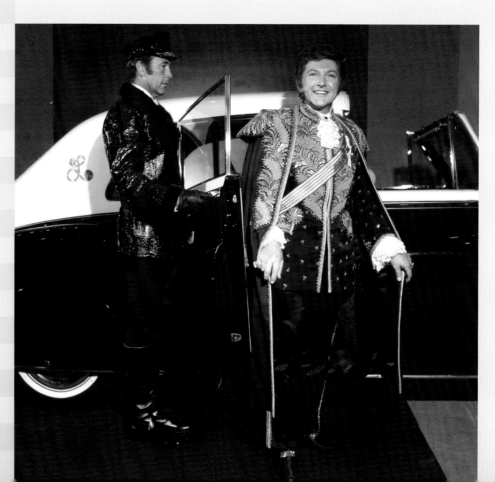

"My clothes may look funny, but they're making me the money."

scampi prosciutto

½ cup olive oil

2 garlic cloves, crushed

½ pound prosciutto, thinly sliced

¼ cup tomato paste

¼ cup water

½ cup broth or white wine

1 teaspoon salt

½ teaspoon pepper

½ teaspoon oregano

a pinch of mace

3 pounds raw shrimp, peeled

½ cup chopped parsley

(Italian flat leaf, if available)

Serves 8

Heat the oil in a deep skillet, add the garlic and the prosciutto cut into julienne strips.

Cook for 3 minutes over low heat being careful not to brown.

Add the tomato paste, ¼ cup water and the broth or wine.

Season with salt, pepper, oregano and mace.

Add the shrimp and simmer for 5 minutes, turning the shrimp so all are covered in sauce.

A minute before serving, stir in the parsley and adjust salt to taste.

Serve with rice, risotto or noodles.

"Liberace was the kind of person who would come up to you in the supermarket, poke his head into your shopping cart, and say 'whatcha gonna do with that chicken?'"

RETRO SPAGHETTI WITH MEAT SAUCE

4 tablespoons butter

1 pound ground beef

3 tablespoons fine dry
   breadcrumbs

1¾ cups tomato purée

1 six-ounce can tomato paste

1 tablespoon onion powder

1 garlic clove, crushed

½ teaspoon salt

½ teaspoon basil

½ teaspoon oregano

½ teaspoon sugar

1 pound spaghetti

grated Parmesan cheese

Melt 2 tablespoons butter in a large skillet and sauté the beef.

When browned, add the remaining butter, breadcrumbs, tomato purée and tomato paste with 1 can (six-ounce tomato paste can) of hot water, onion powder, garlic, salt, basil, oregano and sugar.

Cover and simmer for about 20 minutes.

Meanwhile, cook the spaghetti according to package directions.

Drain the spaghetti, rinse with boiling water.

Serve mixed with meat sauce and top with cheese.

"I didn't get dressed like this to go unnoticed."

1 pound spaghetti

salt

1 tablespoon olive oil

¼ pound butter

2 tablespoons hot heavy cream

½ cup grated Parmesan cheese

Serves 4 to 6

Cook the spaghetti in 4 to 5 quarts of boiling salted water to which you have added the olive oil. Drain.

You have to work fast so the spaghetti is steaming when you dress it.

Cut up the butter and put it on the spaghetti with cream and ¼ cup of cheese. Toss.

Sprinkle the remaining cheese on top.

spaghetti parmesan

1 pound spaghetti

½ cup grated Parmesan cheese

¼ cup melted butter

1 teaspoon salt

¼ cup heavy cream

1 garlic clove, crushed

Serves 6

Cook the spaghetti according to package directions. Don't overcook. Drain and rinse with hot or boiling water.

Put the spaghetti into a large bowl, add the remaining ingredients and toss well.

Serve immediately.

We are gathered here today

Recipes designed to win friends and influence people

Liberace used his ample earnings to purchase all the beautiful things he could. And, since shopping was his hobby, he managed to buy quite a lot. He used these treasures to entertain his guests at the highest level possible. These recipes are the crème de la crème when asking the boss for a raise, entertaining critics or hosting your neighborhood block party. All are designed for flawless execution of the axiom that anything worth doing is well worth overdoing. And, of course, such Liberace elegance will certainly help anyone's culinary repertoire strike a high note. It doesn't matter if your dream is to make it huge in entertainment or just to make it huge, these dishes will fit the bill. They'll be the talk of the office water cooler—and that's no bologna.

"Mother was a good cook, but a limited one, strictly a roast chicken, pot roast and potatoes type."

2 grapefruit, peeled and
sectioned

4 oranges, peeled and sectioned

4 peaches, cut up

2 cups cut-up fresh pineapple

2 cups diced melon

1 cup seedless grapes

½ cup mayonnaise

1 teaspoon lemon juice

1 teaspoon orange juice

1 teaspoon pineapple juice

1 teaspoon sugar

½ cup whipped cream

Serves 8

Mix the fruit together in a cold serving bowl.

Mix mayonnaise with remaining ingredients and toss in a bowl with fruit.

Liberace was eulogized in *Time* as "a synonym for glorious excess." The writer continued, "Liberace was a visual, rather than an acoustic phenomenon. He chartered a path followed by the unlikeliest of protégés, from Elvis Presley to Elton John and Boy George. The sex idol as peacock androgyne."

i-DID-IT-MY-way cucumbers in cream

4 large cucumbers

salt

2 red onions, thinly sliced
    into rings

3 teaspoons sugar

½ cup heavy cream

½ teaspoon freshly ground pepper

¼ cup vinegar

Serves 8

Peel cucumbers and score with the prongs of a fork, then cut into thin slices.

Put into a large bowl in layers and sprinkle each layer with salt.

Cover with a plate and weight it down. Let stand at least several hours.

Rinse cucumbers thoroughly and drain.

Combine onion rings with cucumbers.

Mix the sugar, cream and pepper and stir in the vinegar.

Pour over the cucumbers.

Big shot cheese straws

¼ cup shortening

1 cup flour

1 cup grated Cheddar cheese

½ teaspoon salt

1 egg

2 tablespoons ice water

paprika

Makes 18

Preheat oven to 400 degrees (F).

Cut shortening into flour and add cheese and salt, mixing well.

Beat egg well with ice water and add to the cheese mixture.

Roll out on a lightly floured board to ⅛-inch thickness.

Cut into narrow strips 4 inches long and dust with paprika.

Place on a greased baking sheet and bake about 10 minutes, or until crisp and golden brown.

THERE'S-NO-PLACE-LIKE-HOME POTATO SOUP
(MOM'S BLUE-RIBBON RECIPE)

3 large potatoes, peeled and diced

salt

2 quarts water

¼ pound thin noodles

¼ pound thickly sliced bacon,
    diced

1 large onion, chopped

¼ teaspoon white pepper

Cook the potatoes in 2 quarts of salted water.

Cook the noodles according to package instructions.

Combine noodles with the potatoes and their liquid.

Meanwhile, sauté the bacon with the onion. Stir into soup.

Add pepper and season to taste.

CRAB COCKTAIL

4 pounds of crab meat
    (Dungeness, king or
    California crab legs)

2 cups mayonnaise

1 tablespoon lemon juice

1 tablespoon minced parsley
    or watercress

1 tablespoon curry powder
    (optional)

lemon wedges

Serves 12

Mix mayonnaise with lemon juice and parsley or watercress;
add curry if desired.

Place crab in sherbet glasses or arranged on individual dishes
over beds of cracked ice.

Top each serving with a small amount of the sauce.

Serve with lemon wedges.

1 teaspoon sugar

1 teaspoon butter

1 cup flour

½ cup milk

2 eggs, beaten

pinch of salt

pinch of nutmeg

2 large McIntosh apples,
    peeled and coarsely
    chopped

fat for frying

Serves 4 to 6

Mix the sugar, butter, flour and milk.

Add the eggs, salt and nutmeg, and beat well.

The batter should be thicker than pancake batter.

Stir in the apples.

Fry in about a half inch of hot fat.

When Liberace was a child, his mother
Frances worked in a cookie factory to
help support the family.

6 large potatoes

2 large onions, thinly sliced

2 sweet pickles, chopped

1 cup diced celery

1 teaspoon salt

¼ teaspoon pepper

6 slices bacon, diced

2 tablespoons flour

¼ cup water

¼ cup white vinegar

2 tablespoons olive oil

1 tablespoon sugar

2 tablespoons chopped parsley

Serves 6

Cook potatoes about 25 minutes until soft but not mushy.

Rinse in cold water, peel, and thinly slice into large bowl.

Add onion, pickle, celery, salt and pepper and toss gently.

Sauté the bacon until crisp, remove the pieces with a slotted spoon, and add to the potatoes.

Pour off all but 2 tablespoons of bacon drippings, add flour, heat and blend well.

Add ¼ cup water as mixture thickens.

Add vinegar, oil and sugar and bring to a boil.

Add sauce to potatoes and toss gently.

Sprinkle with parsley and serve salad warm or cold.

"When it came to opening night, my mother would say, 'Well, *you* pick something for me to wear.'"

3 tablespoons butter

½ pound mushrooms, sliced

1 tablespoon minced onion

1 cup chicken broth

4 cups ½-inch pieces of cut

    celery

2 teaspoons soy sauce

½ teaspoon salt

¼ teaspoon pepper

¾ cup grated Parmesan cheese

buttered crumbs

Serves 6

Preheat oven to 350 degrees (F).

Heat butter and sauté the mushrooms and onion 3 minutes.

Bring broth to a simmer, add celery and cook until tender.

Put mushroom mixture and celery with broth into a casserole with soy sauce, salt, pepper and ½ cup of cheese.

Mix until heated through and brown on top.

Liberace's mother puts her feet up while her cookies are in the oven . . .

salamiami bouquet

1 tablespoon cream

1 eight-ounce package cream cheese, softened

½ pound salami (about 4- to 6-inch diameter), sliced paper thin

Serves 8

Mix cream with cream cheese.

Spread a little of the mixture on each slice of salami.

Cut in half.

Roll up and fasten with a decorative toothpick.

Liberace's trademark smooth and deliberate speaking style resulted from childhood sessions with a speech therapist. The lessons were necessary to eliminate the effects of listening to one parent who spoke with an Italian accent and another with a Polish accent.

steak tartare

2 pounds filet or sirloin of beef

2 egg yolks

2 teaspoons minced onion

1 tablespoon Worcestershire
    sauce

1 teaspoon salt

¼ teaspoon of freshly ground
    pepper

anchovies

capers

minced parsley

Serves 8 to 10 for canapés

Have your meat cutter trim all the fat from the beef, then have beef ground twice.

Mix beef with egg yolks, onion, Worcestershire sauce, salt and pepper. Toss lightly and season to taste.

Form mixture into a loaf, and garnish with the anchovies.

Serve sprinkled with capers and parsley and accompany with toast or crackers.

(WARNING: Science has taught us that raw meat and uncooked eggs can be hazardous to your health these days, plus they aren't too gastro-nomically appealing anymore. Liberace probably wouldn't recommend this one in today's world. Consider this a "read-only" delight, a recipe included only for history's sake, not for eating . . .)

The real Lord of the Rings.

chicken in brandy and cream
(less is definitely not more)

2 three-pound frying chickens,
cut up

2 teaspoons salt

¼ teaspoon white pepper

¼ cup butter

2 large garlic cloves, split

¼ cup brandy, warmed

¼ cup water

1 cup dry white wine

3 egg yolks

1½ cups heavy cream

Serves 8

Rub the chickens with a mixture of salt and pepper.

Heat butter and brown chickens with garlic, adding more butter if necessary to prevent sticking.

Stir to brown chicken pieces thoroughly on all sides.

Remove garlic.

Add the warmed brandy and ignite. Shake the pan until the brandy burns out.

Add ¼ cup water and white wine and simmer, covered, for 15 minutes.

Transfer chicken to a heated platter and keep warm.

Beat egg yolks into cream and pour into the pan drippings.

Simmer and stir gently until thickened.

Pour over chicken.

*"Nobody will believe in you
unless you believe in yourself."*

chicken liver paté

1 fourteen-ounce can chicken
   broth or consommé

1 envelope unflavored gelatin

¼ cup Madeira, port or brandy

2 tablespoons butter

3 tablespoons minced onion

1 pound chicken livers, cut up

½ pound liver sausage

1 teaspoon salt

¼ teaspoon freshly ground pepper

½ teaspoon marjoram

¼ teaspoon oregano

1 tablespoon Worcestershire
   sauce

2 hard-boiled eggs, grated

Serves 8 to 10

Heat broth and add a little to the gelatin; stir to dissolve.

Add the remaining broth and 2 tablespoons of the liquor of your choice.

Pour ⅓ of the mixture into the bottom of a mold or bowl.

Refrigerate and keep remaining broth at room temperature.

Melt butter and sauté onion 2 minutes.

Add livers and cook very gently for about 5 minutes.

They should not brown.

Add the liver sausage and heat until softened.

Remove from heat and season with salt, pepper, marjoram, oregano
and Worcestershire sauce.

Add remaining 2 tablespoons liquor.

Put 3 tablespoons of broth into blender container, add livers and blend
at lowest speed. Mixture should remain lumpy.

Stir in grated eggs.

When the layer of gelatin in the mold has set, place liver mixture on it,
leaving a little space around the sides.

Pour remaining broth around the sides and over the top.

Refrigerate several hours until firm.

Serve with toast or crackers.

RUSSIAN SALAD
(TCHAIKOVSKY LOVED THIS SALAD!)

3 cups diced cooked beef or chicken

½ cup diced cooked ham

½ cup diced cooked beets

1 cup diced, peeled, cooked potatoes

½ cup thinly sliced dill pickle spears

1 cucumber, peeled and diced

2 hard-boiled eggs, chopped

2 tablespoons chopped black olives

1 cup canned kidney beans, drained

1 cup sauerkraut, drained

½ cup French dressing

½ teaspoon prepared mustard

Serves 8

Combine all ingredients.

Mix the French dressing with mustard and pour over salad.

Toss well.

The tables were always set in Liberace's homes.

you'll-Thank-me-Later codfish cakes

2 cups shredded cooked codfish

2 cups mashed potatoes

2 eggs, slightly beaten

¼ teaspoon pepper

fat for frying

Serves 4

Mix codfish, potatoes, eggs and pepper.

Form into small balls or cakes of about 1 tablespoon each and immerse in 380-degree (F) fat.

Fry cakes a few at a time until golden brown.

Drain on paper towels.

Baked shrimp with whiskey
(THis Dish'll make even crotchety uncle edward crack a grin)

3 pounds raw shrimp

½ teaspoon salt

1 teaspoon freshly ground pepper

¼ cup melted butter

2 tablespoons lemon juice

⅓ cup whiskey

Serves 6

Preheat broiler to medium broil.

Peel the shrimp. Arrange in broiling pan.

Mix salt and pepper with butter and lemon juice and pour over the shrimp. Turn to be sure they're coated on both sides.

Broil about 4 inches from heat until they turn pink—not more than 3 minutes.

Pour the whiskey over, reduce heat and cook 5 more minutes.

Serve with rice, buttered noodles, spaghetti or on toasted white bread.

POOFY PUFFY SPUDS

3 cups mashed potatoes

3 eggs, beaten

¾ teaspoon salt

½ teaspoon baking powder

1 teaspoon grated onion

½ teaspoon nutmeg

deep fat for frying

Serves 8

Mix potatoes with remaining ingredients.

Heat deep fat to 380 degrees (F).

Drop potato mixture by spoonfuls into fat and fry until golden.

Drain on paper towels.

Liberace is included in *Ripley's Believe It or Not* for being able to play six thousand notes in under two minutes.

2 celery hearts

celery

¼ pound blue Roquefort cheese

¼ pound unsalted butter

1 teaspoon prepared mustard

2 tablespoons Worcestershire
    sauce

paprika

Serves 6

Wash celery. Remove the small center pieces, leaving the leaves on.
Scrape the outside pieces, then split and cut them into 4-inch lengths.
Blend the cheese and butter with mustard and Worcestershire sauce.
Fill the stalks and sprinkle with paprika.

Variation: Substitute 1 three-ounce package of cream cheese for the
butter and add 1 tablespoon mayonnaise, cream or sour cream.

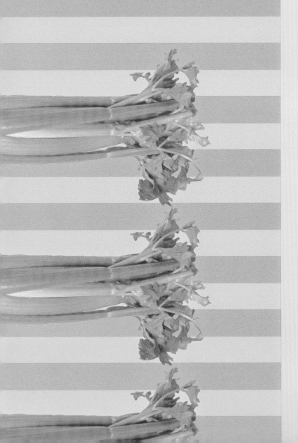

Liberace flanked by two fans.

1 one pound can kidney beans

3 cups cut green beans or

2 packages frozen

3 cups fresh baby lima beans

or 2 packages frozen

salt

1 cup chopped celery

1 Bermuda onion or

4 green onions, chopped

1 tablespoon sugar

½ cup French dressing

salad greens

Serves 12 to 15

Rinse the kidney beans and drain.

Cook the green beans and lima beans in salted water until tender.
If using frozen, follow package directions.

Drain and mix with the kidney beans, celery and onion.

Add the sugar to the French dressing and toss gently with the beans.

Serve garnished with salad greens.

turkey tetrazzini

¾ pound spaghetti or elbow
macaroni

1½ cups chicken broth

1½ cups water

¼ cup butter

1 pound mushrooms, sliced

1 garlic clove, minced or crushed

3 tablespoons flour

⅓ cup heavy cream

3 cups diced or cut-up
cooked turkey

⅓ cup grated Parmesan cheese

Serves 6

Preheat oven to 450 degrees (F).

Cook the spaghetti in half broth and half water for about
10 minutes or until barely tender. Drain, reserving liquid.

Heat half the butter and sauté mushrooms and garlic, remove from
pan and stir in the flour.

Stir in 2½ cups of reserved liquid and the cream.

Cook and stir until smooth and thickened.

Put a layer of half of the spaghetti in the bottom of a large greased
casserole or baking dish.

Cover with half the mushrooms and half the turkey.

Pour over half the sauce and sprinkle with half the cheese.

Repeat, ending with cream sauce on top.

Sprinkle with remaining cheese.

Bake until bubbly and very lightly browned.

Even a casual
dinner on the
deck gets the
Liberace treat-
ment complete
with silver and
fine china.

decorative crab balls

1 pound crab meat

1 tablespoon butter

1 tablespoon minced onion

¼ cup breadcrumbs

2 eggs, beaten

½ teaspoon salt

⅛ teaspoon pepper

1 tablespoon minced parsley

flour or fine breadcrumbs

deep fat for frying

Serves 12

Pick over the crab meat.

Heat butter and sauté onion until transparent.

Mix with the crab, adding crumbs, eggs, salt, pepper and parsley.

Form into small balls and roll them in flour or breadcrumbs.

Heat fat to 375 degrees (F) and fry crab balls, a few at a time, 2 or 3 minutes until brown.

"Don't wear one ring, wear five or six. People ask how I can play with all those rings, and I reply, 'Very well, thank you.'"

SUCCULENT SUCCOTASH

12 ears of corn or 3 packages frozen

¼ cup butter

4 cups fresh lima beans or 3 packages frozen

1 cup half-and-half or cream

½ teaspoon sugar

½ teaspoon salt

¼ teaspoon pepper

Serves 12

Cut corn from the cob and cook in butter for 3 minutes.

Cook the beans until tender, drain and combine with the corn. If using frozen, cook according to package directions, drain, combine and add butter.

Add half-and-half, sugar, salt and pepper, and heat but don't boil.

"Isn't this a fun place?"

—*Liberace, speaking about his home*

sweet-n-sauerkraut

2 one-pound, eleven-ounce cans
sauerkraut

3 apples, peeled, cored and
chopped

1 tablespoon caraway seed

1½ cups dry white wine

½ cup beef broth

1 teaspoon sugar

½ teaspoon salt

Serves 12

Rinse the sauerkraut thoroughly.

Bring large pot of water to a boil, add sauerkraut, then drain.

Combine cabbage with the remaining ingredients and simmer, covered, for half an hour.

If the sauerkraut seems too moist, sprinkle with a tablespoon or two of flour for the last 5 minutes of cooking.

Candelabra were de rigueur
at any Liberace table.

sukiyaki-a-go-go

2 tablespoons peanut oil or butter

1 pound of lean tender beef or

pork, very thinly cut

2 large onions, sliced

1 garlic clove, minced

1 bunch green onions,

shredded lengthwise

1 medium cauliflower,

finely shredded

1 one-pound can bean sprouts,

drained

2 green peppers, seeded and

shredded

¼ cup sugar

1 teaspoon salt

¼ cup sake or sherry

1 teaspoon monosodium glutamate

or substitute (optional)

1 tablespoon flour or cornstarch

2 or 3 tablespoons broth

bean curd and/or rice

Serves 8

Heat oil or butter in large skillet and sauté beef for 1 minute.
If using pork, cook 3 minutes.

Brown onions, garlic and green onions in same skillet for 2 to
3 minutes.

Add cauliflower, bean sprouts and green peppers, stir and cook
2 minutes.

Sprinkle with sugar and salt, add the soy, sake or sherry,
monosodium glutamate if desired, and flour dissolved in the broth.

Cook 2 minutes.

Serve with bean curd and/or rice.

Sukiyaki must be eaten immediately while the vegetables are crisp.

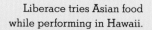

Liberace tries Asian food
while performing in Hawaii.

it's-what's-inside-that-counts pot roast

1 four- to-five-pound chuck,
  round or sirloin tip roast

2 teaspoons salt

½ teaspoon pepper

2 tablespoons flour

3 tablespoons oil or butter

2 tablespoons chopped onion

1 garlic clove, crushed

1 cup wine or wine vinegar

1 cup water or broth

1 teaspoon fines herbes

6 cloves

1 bay leaf

1 teaspoon sugar

flour

vegetables, such as carrots,
  turnips, small onions, diced
  celery, green peppers and
  potatoes

Serves 8

Rub the meat with salt and pepper and dredge with flour.

Heat oil or butter in a deep casserole and brown meat on all sides.

Add the onion and garlic while browning.

Pour in the liquid, add fines herbes, cloves, bay leaf and sugar and simmer covered for 2 to 2½ hours or until tender.

Add vegetables during the last half hour of cooking.

Remove meat to a warm platter.

Remove fat from juices in casserole, add a little flour mixed with enough water to form a paste and cook for 3 to 4 minutes.

Return mixture to casserole.

Cut meat into serving pieces and return to casserole.

chicken à la king of bling!

¼ cup butter

3 tablespoons chopped pimiento

3 tablespoons chopped
   green pepper

¼ pound mushrooms, sliced

3 tablespoons flour

1 cup chicken broth

1 cup heavy cream

1 teaspoon salt

3 cups cut-up cooked chicken

3 egg yolks

3 tablespoons sherry

Serves 6

Heat 3 tablespoons butter and sauté the pimiento and green pepper for 4 minutes.

Add mushrooms and cook 3 minutes.

Push the vegetables aside and stir in the flour.

Add broth, while stirring, and cream and salt.

Simmer until thickened and add the chicken to heat through.

Beat egg yolks with a little cream or broth and stir in.

Cook gently, stirring, for 2 to 3 minutes.

Add sherry and drizzle the remaining butter over chicken mixture just just prior to serving.

Serve in patty shells, on toast, rolls or on rice.

Liberace wore his platinum suit long before Elvis wore his gold tuxedo, but who's counting?

super-swingin' sweet potatoes

9 to 10 sweet potatoes, peeled

salt

½ cup orange juice

3 teaspoons grated orange rind

⅓ cup butter

2 eggs, beaten

1½ teaspoons salt

3 tablespoons hot cream

10 to 12 marshmallows

Serves 10 to 12

Preheat oven to 350 degrees (F).

Cut up the sweet potatoes and cook in salted water until soft. Drain.

Mix with orange juice, orange rind, butter, eggs, salt and cream.

Whip until light and fluffy.

Put into a greased baking dish and push the marshmallows into the top until half buried.

Bake about half an hour until thoroughly heated through and the marshmallows are browned.

FLASHY FISH CASSEROLE

3 pounds fish fillets (cod,

    haddock or flounder)

4 potatoes, peeled and thinly

    sliced

2 onions, thinly sliced

1 bay leaf

2 teaspoons salt

½ teaspoon white pepper

1 cup dry white wine

½ cup water

¼ pound butter

2 cups cream

2 egg yolks

Serves 6 to 8

Preheat oven to 350 degrees (F).

Put the fish fillets in a greased casserole with potatoes, onions, bay leaf, salt, pepper, wine and water.

Bake half an hour.

Add butter and bake another 15 minutes.

Mix cream with egg yolks in a small pan, bring to a boil and add to the casserole.

piece o'cake potato pancakes

3 large potatoes, peeled and grated

2 onions, grated

2 tablespoons flour

2 eggs, beaten

1 teaspoon salt

¼ teaspoon pepper

Crisco or lard for frying

Serves 6

Mix the grated potatoes and onions and drain off excess liquid.

Stir in the flour, eggs, salt and pepper.

Heat about an inch of Crisco or lard in large frying pan.

Drop tablespoon-sized potato mixture into fat, browning each side.

Drain on paper towels.

Liberace never stopped
tinkling the ivories!

weenie broil

16 frankfurters

(or 8 knockwurst)

prepared mustard

butter

bacon

Serves 8

Slash franks, grill over moderate coals and turn so they don't char.

Cut light gashes and fill with mustard or mustard mixed with soft butter.

Wrap bacon around each, fasten with a toothpick, and finish grilling.

Serve with or without rolls.

*"I love seeing beautifully set tables.
In my own homes,
the tables are always set,
even if I'm not expecting guests."*

Liberace gives the table in his Hollywood den a last once-over before an intimate dinner party.

divine turkey divan

2 pounds asparagus or

1 large bunch of broccoli

cooked turkey breast, sliced

3 tablespoons butter

3 tablespoons flour

1½ cups half-and-half or milk

1 teaspoon salt

¼ teaspoon pepper

½ cup grated Parmesan cheese

Serves 6

Cook asparagus (or broccoli) in salted water until tender.

Meanwhile, prepare sauce. Heat butter and stir in flour. (Wondra flour makes a smoother sauce.)

Slowly add half-and-half while stirring.

Add salt and pepper and cook until smooth and thick.

Add half the grated cheese and stir until melted.

Drain vegetables and transfer to large shallow greased baking dish.

Cover completely with sliced turkey.

Preheat broiler.

Pour sauce over top of casserole, cover with remaining cheese, and put under broiler until Turkey Divan is bubbly and lightly browned on top.

NOODLES WITH COTTAGE CHEESE

1 pound medium noodles

salt

1 pound cottage cheese

1 pint sour cream

½ cup grated Parmesan cheese

2 tablespoons butter

Serves 6

Preheat oven to 350 degrees (F).

Cook the noodles in boiling salted water for 12 minutes. Drain.

Put a layer of noodles in the bottom of a greased baking dish, then a layer of cheese, and then sour cream.

Sprinkle with Parmesan cheese and repeat layers. End with Parmesan cheese on top and dot with butter.

Bake 20 minutes.

Liberace enjoyed being recognized in public and always agreed to autographs with two exceptions. "If I'm having dinner, I ask them to return after I've finished eating. I also refuse to sign when I'm in the men's room."

Well, what do you think, too much?

Dishes that take the road-less-traveled

Even the road-less-traveled was too congested for Liberace. Since there was no signpost alerting him to stop—he just didn't bother. Whether he was making Flamboyant Flambé of Sirloin or Livers in Champagne, decadence in flavor and presentation was a Liberace trademark.

These are dinner recipes designed to *create* special notice not only for the execution, but also for the ingredients. For example, it isn't every day that most folks serve oxtail, regardless of the preparation. But why not, Liberace would ask, why not? Unusual combinations make for unusual people. *Viva* the Liberaces of the world!

Bling and more Bling— Liberace always sparkled.

eggs with caviar

8 hard-boiled eggs

3 tablespoons soft butter

2 tablespoons vinegar

½ teaspoon salt

½ teaspoon sugar

½ teaspoon dry mustard

2 teaspoons onion juice

½ teaspoon lemon juice

4 ounces red caviar

minced chives

Serves 6 to 8

Cut eggs in half lengthwise.

Put the yolks into a bowl and mix with butter, vinegar, salt, sugar, mustard, onion and lemon juices.

Blend well and gently stir in half the caviar. Be careful not to break the caviar eggs.

Fill the egg whites with yolk mixture and top each with a dollop of caviar and a sprinkling of chives.

Nothing that costs a dollar is worth eating, so add caviar

Liberace *loved* dogs and owned twenty-six at one point.

way-over-the-top caviar cheese dip

1 eight-ounce package cream cheese

3 tablespoons whipping cream or
  sour cream

2 tablespoons minced chives or
  onion

2 tablespoons lemon juice

1 tablespoon Worcestershire sauce

3 tablespoons red caviar

paprika

Makes about 1 cup

Blend the cheese and cream.

Add chives, lemon juice and Worcestershire sauce and mix well.

Stir in the red caviar, transfer to a serving bowl, and sprinkle the top with a pinch of paprika.

Serve with crackers.

precocious pumpkin soup

½ medium pumpkin or 3 cups

canned pumpkin purée

1 quart water

2 teaspoons salt

¼ cup butter

1 teaspoon sugar

¼ teaspoon white pepper

1 quart milk

Serves 6

Cut up the pumpkin flesh and boil until tender in just enough salted water to cover.

Force through a sieve or purée in a blender.

You will need about 3 cups of mixture.

Combine the purée, butter, sugar and pepper in a pan and simmer for 10 minutes.

Pour in the milk and simmer for 3 minutes more.

Season to taste.

luminous lemon soup

6 cups chicken broth

½ cup uncooked rice

3 eggs, beaten

3 tablespoons lemon juice

½ cup sour cream (optional)

Heat broth, add rice and cook 20 minutes.

Whisk eggs with lemon juice, pour in a little hot broth while whisking, return mixture to soup, stir and heat until slightly thickened.

Add the sour cream just prior to serving if desired.

6 large artichokes

salt

6 tablespoons butter

5 tablespoons flour

1 teaspoon salt

a pinch of nutmeg

1 quart cream or half-and-half

1 cup dry white wine

Serves 6 to 8

Cook the artichokes in salted water until very soft. Reserve liquid.

Separate artichoke leaves, remove thorns and scrape the ends off the leaves, adding scrapings to the fonds (bottoms).

Mash thoroughly or purée in a blender with 1 cup of reserved liquid.

Melt 4 tablespoons of butter in medium pan, blend with the flour, and add the artichoke mixture, salt and nutmeg.

Simmer for 3 minutes.

Stir in the cream or half-and-half and reheat.

Just prior to serving, stir in the wine slowly and add the remaining butter while stirring.

"My physical fitness instructor tells me I have the legs of an athlete."

jellied clamato garni

4 packages of unflavored gelatin

2½ quarts Clamato

juice of one lemon

6 ounces red caviar or

    6 tablespoons minced clams

1 cup sour cream

minced chives or parsley

lemon wedges

Serves 12

Soften the gelatin in Clamato and heat to dissolve. Cool.

Stir in the lemon juice and caviar or clams.

Divide soup into 12 soup cups.

Chill until firm.

Top each with 1 tablespoon sour cream and chives or parsley.

Serve with lemon wedges.

jellied madrilène

Follow recipe for Jellied Clamato but substitute 5 thirteen-ounce cans of chilled madrilène for Clamato. Omit the caviar and clams and proceed as for Jellied Clamato Garni.

POLISH RADISH SALAD

3 bunches radishes

½ teaspoon salt

½ teaspoon freshly ground pepper

2 hard-boiled eggs

Sassy Sour Cream Sauce

(see recipe below)

Wash, trim and thinly slice radishes into rounds.

Add salt and pepper.

Finely chop egg whites and mix yolks with ½ cup of Sassy Sour Cream Sauce.

Blend radishes and sauce and garnish with chopped egg whites.

You can choose to tint the radishes the way our chefs from the Riviera Hotel and Casino did for the picture at right.

sassy sour cream sauce

½ cup sour cream

½ teaspoon salt

1/16 teaspoon white pepper

¼ teaspoon sugar

⅛ cup white wine vinegar

1 tablespoon minced olives

Mix all the ingredients together.

opposites-attract orange-onion salad

6 to 8 oranges

1 large sweet onion, thinly sliced

½ pound black seedless olives

½ cup Lemon French Dressing

greens

pimiento, cut into strips

Serves 6 to 8

Peel and thinly slice oranges.

Mix oranges, onion and olives and add the Lemon French dressing.

Let stand for an hour.

Tossing repeatedly, place on greens and garnish with pimiento.

lemon french dressing

¼ cup lemon juice

1 teaspoon salt

¼ teaspoon pepper

½ teaspoon sugar

¾ cup olive oil

Makes 1 cup

Mix the lemon juice with salt, pepper and sugar.

Add oil slowly—1 tablespoon at a time while stirring. If using on fruit salad, decrease the amount of salt to ½ teaspoon and increase the sugar to 1 teaspoon.

HALCYON DAYS
GRAPEFRUIT AND AVOCADO SALAD

3 avocados

2 tablespoons lemon juice

4 grapefruit, peeled and sectioned

soft greens or watercress

1 eight-ounce package cream cheese

paprika

¾ cup Lemon French dressing

Serves 6

Peel the avocados, cut in half and then slice.

Sprinkle at once with lemon juice to prevent discoloring.

Place alternate slices of avocado and grapefruit sections on a bed of the greens or watercress.

Roll the cheese into balls and sprinkle with paprika.

Place cheese balls around the salad and pour the dressing over.

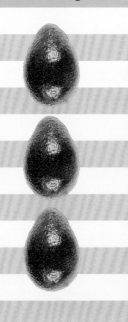

Little Richard nicknamed himself "The Bronze Liberace."

MUSHROOMS STUFFED WITH SARDINES

1 pound small mushrooms

1 three-ounce package cream
cheese

2 teaspoons lemon juice

1 three-and-one-half-ounce can
skinless, boneless sardines,
drained

2 teaspoons chives or scallions,
minced

½ teaspoon salt

dash pepper

2 tablespoons cream (about)

Serves 6 to 8

Remove the stems from the mushrooms and peel the caps by grasping the edge and pulling gently across the top.

Mix the cream cheese, lemon juice, sardines, chives or scallions, salt and pepper.

Stir in cream to desired consistency.

Chopped anchovies may be substituted for sardines, in which case, omit salt.

Stuff the caps with the mixture.

Liberace and fan Jack Goldman.

POLISH SAUERKRAUT CASSEROLE

1 pound lean pork, cut into pieces

1 pound bulk pork sausage

2 onions, chopped

2 apples, peeled, cored, diced

½ cup tomato purée

2 tablespoons meat paste or 2 bouillon cubes

1 teaspoon sugar

¼ teaspoon pepper

½ cup water

2 pounds sauerkraut

Serves 6

Preheat oven to 350 degrees (F).

Fry the pork and sausage in large skillet until well browned.

Add the onions, apples, tomato purée, meat paste or bouillon cubes, sugar, pepper and ½ cup water.

Wash, drain and stir in the sauerkraut.

Put in a 2-quart casserole, cover tightly, and bake about 1½ hours.

Stir occasionally and add a little water if needed.

creamed spinach with nutmeg

8 pounds of spinach or

    6 packages of frozen

½ cup butter

¼ cup flour

1½ teaspoons salt

½ teaspoon pepper

½ to 1 teaspoon nutmeg

1 cup cream

Serves 10 to 12

Wash the spinach, changing the water several times.

Cook for a few minutes with just the water that clings to the leaves until the spinach is thoroughly wilted. Drain well, reserving ½ cup liquid. If using frozen spinach, cook according to package instructions until just soft, reserving ½ cup liquid.

Press through a coarse sieve or purée in blender.

Melt the butter and blend in the flour.

Add the seasonings and reserved liquid.

Stir in the cream and cook, stirring constantly, until thickened.

Add the puréed spinach, mix and heat thoroughly.

chicken liver and caper canapé

1 tablespoon butter

3 tablespoons minced onion

¼ cup chicken broth

2 tablespoons white wine

½ teaspoon salt

1 pound chicken livers, finely

    chopped

1 to 1½ tablespoons capers,

    drained

Serves 5

Heat butter and sauté the onion until transparent.

Add the broth and simmer for 2 minutes.

Add the wine, salt and livers and cook, stirring, for 5 minutes.

Remove from heat and add capers. Chill.

Serve with crackers, toast or thin dark bread.

1 pound chicken livers

3 tablespoons flour

1 teaspoon salt

¼ cup butter

¼ cup chopped onion

4 scallions, minced

1 garlic clove, crushed

¾ cup chicken broth or water

1 cup champagne

Serves 4

Dust the chicken livers with flour and salt. The easiest way is to shake them in a paper bag.

Heat the butter and sauté the onion for 3 minutes.

Add the scallions, garlic, livers and cook 5 minutes, stirring gently.

Add a little more butter if necessary.

Pour in the broth or water, then the champagne and cook 1 minute more until hot.

"I'm half Italian and half Polish . . . (applause) . . . Thank you from both halves."

secret weapon casserole

3 pounds squid

¼ cup olive oil

4 shallots, minced, or

    ¼ cup chopped onion

¼ cup parsley

¼ cup minced celery

chopped celery leaves

1 garlic clove

1 teaspoon salt

¼ teaspoon pepper

¼ teaspoon thyme or oregano

2 tablespoons tomato paste or

    ¼ cup red wine

Serves 6

Clean the squid by removing the head and the transparent spine.

Wash the body thoroughly and rub off the thin outside skin. Save the ink if possible.

Cut up the tentacles and cut the body into ½-inch rings.

Heat oil and sauté the shallots or onion, parsley, celery, leaves and garlic for several minutes.

Add salt, pepper, thyme or oregano and tomato paste or red wine.

Put the squid and any ink into the mixture and simmer until tender.

If the squid is very young, it can take 10 minutes, but it can also take an hour.

Serve with rice.

Liberace set the standard for the glitz and glamour now synonymous with Las Vegas, Nevada.

celery victor/victoria

8 celery hearts or 4 heads of

    Pascal celery

consommé or beef broth

watercress or leaf lettuce

1 cup vinaigrette dressing

Serves 6

Wash and trim the ends of the celery. If using hearts, leave whole, if large heads, remove a few outside leaves and cut the head in half.

Cook the celery in consommé or other broth until tender.

Let cool in the broth. Don't overcook; it will continue to cook in the broth after it's removed from heat.

Drain and chill.

Serve on a bed of greens.

Stir the dressing and drizzle over the salad.

BLissFUL Broccoli WiTH Olives

3 pounds broccoli

salt

¼ cup olive oil

1 garlic clove, minced

1 teaspoon lemon juice

1 cup minced ripe olives or

    1½ cups sliced

½ teaspoon salt

¼ teaspoon pepper

Serves 6 to 8

Cook broccoli in salted water until tender but not mushy.

Heat olive oil and sauté the garlic.

Add lemon juice and olives.

Drain the broccoli and place in a heated dish.

Sprinkle with salt and pepper, and pour the sauce over.

STUFFED SQUID

4 pounds baby squid

1 teaspoon salt

1½ cups chopped parsley

½ cup breadcrumbs

minced flesh of 1 large tomato

2 garlic cloves, crushed

2 shallots, minced, or

    2 tablespoons minced chives

    or scallions

6 tablespoons olive oil

Clean the squid. Remove the tentacles and set aside. Cut off the head and take out the transparent spine. Wash the body under running water and remove the outside skin, which peels off easily.

Chop the tentacles coarsely and put into a bowl with the salt, parsley, crumbs, tomato, garlic and shallots.

Moisten with 2 or 3 tablespoons of olive oil.

Fill the bodies loosely with the stuffing and place on an oiled pan.

Sprinkle remaining oil over the squid.

Bake in a 350-degree (F) oven for 10 to 15 minutes until squid swell up and are heated through.

"Even in the kitchen, I am never far from a keyboard."

sauerbraten

6 pound piece of sirloin

4 onions

1 tablespoon salt

pepper

grated rind and juice of 1 lemon

2 cups vinegar

2 bay leaves

2 cloves

12 peppercorns

1 teaspoon sugar

2 cups water

2 tablespoons flour

2 tablespoons water

Serves 6 to 8

Rub the beef with 1 onion, minced, salt, pepper and the lemon rind.

Tie the meat into a roll and put into a deep pot.

Boil the vinegar with bay leaves, cloves, peppercorns, sugar, lemon juice and 2 cups of water for 2 or 3 minutes and pour hot over the beef.

Refrigerate overnight or for 24 hours, turning once or twice.

Preheat oven to 350 degrees (F).

Transfer the meat to a heavy casserole, pour the marinade over and add the remaining onions, thinly sliced.

Bake for about an hour until the meat is tender.

Transfer meat to a heated platter and keep warm.

Strain and skim the fat from the juice.

Make a paste of the flour and 2 tablespoons of water and stir in.

Adjust seasoning, adding sugar to taste.

Liberace's beloved housekeeper and cook, Gladys Luckie, and her brother, Gerard, present Liberace with a down-home evening meal. "Often when I'd come home from the road, where I'd been lobstered and prime-ribbed and steaked to death in fancy restaurants, I'd go into the kitchen and say to Gladys, 'You know what I'd really like tonight? Your meat loaf.'"

glazed corned beef

4 pounds of lean brisket of

corned beef

cloves

¾ cup brown sugar

¼ teaspoon dry mustard

¼ cup sherry

Serves 6

Cover the corned beef with water and simmer for 5 hours.

Drain, reserving 2 tablespoons of the corned beef stock.

Preheat oven to 350 degrees (F).

Put beef into a baking dish, pierce the fat and insert cloves.

Mix the sugar, mustard and sherry with the 2 tablespoons of reserved stock.

Pour over the beef, cover, and bake for 45 minutes, basting frequently.

Serve thinly sliced, either hot or cold.

Liberace prepares his dining table.

veni vidi vici braised oxtails

4 oxtails cut into 1 1/2- to
2-inch pieces

1 teaspoon salt

1/2 teaspoon pepper

flour

3 tablespoons olive oil

1 large onion, finely chopped

2 cans beef broth

2 to 3 bay leaves

1/2 teaspoon oregano

sprig(s) parsley

1/2 cup red wine

1 small can tomato paste

8 carrots cut into 1 1/2-inch pieces

12 small white onions

Serves 6

Use only the large ends of the tails, reserving thin ends for soup.

Season the oxtails with salt and pepper and dust with flour.

Heat oil and sauté the onion for 2 minutes.

Add the oxtails and brown thoroughly, turning to brown evenly.

Add the broth, bay leaves, oregano and parsley, and simmer, covered, for an hour.

Add the wine, tomato paste and water equal in amount to the paste.

Simmer for half an hour.

Add carrots and onions and cook until vegetables are tender.

MY Dear Chicken Fricassee

1 five- to six-pound hen, cut into

serving pieces

6 cups water

2 teaspoons salt

1 small pot (six tablespoons)

prepared mustard

16 small potatoes, peeled

1 cup sour cream

Serves 6

Put the chicken into a pot with 6 cups of water, salt and mustard.

Cook, covered, for an hour.

Add potatoes and cook for 20 to 30 minutes until potatoes are done.

Turn off heat and stir in the sour cream.

"In all of my homes, my favorite room is the kitchen."

FLAMBOYANT FLAMBÉ OF SIRLOIN

¼ cup butter

¼ cup minced shallots or scallions

1 teaspoon salt

½ teaspoon freshly ground pepper

2 tablespoons minced parsley

3½ pounds boned, trimmed sirloin

¼ cup cognac

Heat butter and sauté the shallots or scallions in a large skillet until transparent but not brown.

Add salt, pepper and parsley.

Brown the steak under the broiler for 1 minute and transfer to skillet to cook a few minutes longer, letting the steak juices run into the sauce.

Place on a heated platter.

Warm the cognac, pour over the steak and ignite.

Serve flaming.

Razzle Dazzle
Decadence

Desserts fit for a King . . . and queen

In Liberace's desserts, we find inspiration for a whole new tradition—the "Bling Cake" party. Inspired by the New Orleans Mardi Gras custom of the "King Cake" party, during which a host serves a sugary round cake, called a King Cake, with a tiny "Christ the King" plastic baby doll baked inside. The guest who finds the baby doll in his dessert gets to have the next King Cake party.

Want to try Liberace's Bling Cake party? Buy a very faux engagement ring from a craft store—or if you're lucky, find one in a gumball machine. Hide the ring with the Bling in the Bling Cake. The guest who gets the slice of yummy dessert with the sparkler is engaged to throw the next Bling Cake party! And on it goes. Celebrate all the fabulousness that is you—start a Bling Cake tradition in your circle of excess.

In this chapter, you will find the finishing touches you need to crown the perfect Liberace evening.

Liberace celebrates
in his living room.

Biscuit Tortoni

2 cups heavy cream

1 tablespoon instant coffee

¼ cup sugar

1½ cups macaroon crumbs

2 tablespoons sherry

Serves 8

Put ½ cup of cream in a bowl with the coffee and sugar.

Mix 1 cup of macaroon crumbs and sherry and add to the cream.

Stir well.

Whip the remaining cream and fold into the mixture.

Fill individual paper baking cups with mixture and sprinkle with remaining macaroon crumbs.

Freeze until firm.

Large dining table configured to resemble a grand piano set in Liberace's honor at Bimbo's 365 Club, San Francisco.

afternoon delight brandy snaps

½ cup molasses

½ cup butter

1 cup flour

1 teaspoon powdered ginger

⅔ cup plus 2 tablespoons sugar

1 cup heavy cream

1 tablespoon brandy

Makes about 50

Preheat oven to 300 degrees (F).

Heat the molasses to the boiling point, stir in the butter and remove from heat.

Sift the flour with the ginger and ⅔ cup sugar and add gradually to the molasses mixture. Mix well.

Drop half teaspoonfuls about 3 inches apart onto a greased cookie sheet and bake about 12 minutes.

Remove from the sheet one at a time.

While still warm, roll over the handle of a wooden spoon.

Slip off carefully.

Just before serving, whip the cream until stiff, beat in the remaining sugar, and flavor with brandy.

Fill the cookies.

Big Brazen Brownies

3 ounces unsweetened
chocolate

½ cup butter

1½ cups sugar

3 eggs, beaten

1 cup flour

¼ teaspoon baking powder

¼ teaspoon salt

¾ cup coarsely chopped pecans

1 teaspoon vanilla

Makes about 36

Preheat oven to 350 degrees (F).

Melt the chocolate and butter in top of double boiler over simmering hot water.

Transfer chocolate to large bowl.

Stir the sugar gradually into the beaten eggs and add to the chocolate mixture.

Sift flour with baking powder and salt and blend into the chocolate mixture.

Add the pecans and vanilla and pour into a greased 9×9×2-inch pan.

Bake for about 30 minutes.

Cut into shapes and cool on a wire rack.

*" I love to eat,
and my weight fluctuates.
Most of my suits
come in three varieties—
thin, fat and impossible."*

2 teaspoons unflavored gelatin

½ cup cold water

¼ cup lime juice

⅔ cup sugar

3 eggs

grated rind of ½ lime

pinch of salt

baked pie shell

Serves 6 to 8

Mix gelatin with ½ cup of cold water, lime juice and ⅓ cup sugar.

Separate eggs and beat yolks.

Add gelatin mixture to the beaten egg yolks and cook, stirring, until mixture coats a spoon.

Add the lime rind and chill mixture until slightly thickened.

Beat the egg whites with salt until almost stiff and beat in remaining sugar, a tablespoon at a time.

Fold into the lime mixture and pour into the baked pie shell.

Chill.

Blueberry pie

3 cups fresh blueberries or
unsweetened frozen

1 cup sugar

2 tablespoons flour

1 tablespoon lemon juice

pastry for double-crust pie or
2 prepared crusts

1 tablespoon butter

Serves 8

Preheat oven to 450 degrees (F).

Place unbaked crust in pie pan.

Toss the berries with a mixture of sugar and flour.

Sprinkle with lemon juice.

Heap the berries into the center of pie crust.

Dot with butter and cover with top crust or with a lattice top.

Bake 10 minutes at 450 degrees (F), then reduce heat to 350 degrees (F) and bake 20 minutes.

Liberace shakes the hand of a chef from the Beverly Hills Theatre restaurant.

Brawny Austrian Torte

½ cup butter, softened

1½ cups sugar

2 eggs, beaten

¼ cup milk

1 teaspoon vanilla

2⅔ cups flour

2 tablespoons baking powder

1 teaspoon salt

1 cup slivered almonds

1 pint of heavy cream

Serves 8 to 10

Preheat oven to 375 degrees (F).

Beat butter and sugar together.

Stir in eggs, milk and vanilla and beat until smooth.

Sift flour, baking powder and salt together and add gradually to the mixture.

Pour into two buttered 9-inch baking pans.

Sprinkle generously with almonds generously (reserving some almond slices for decoration) and bake 10 minutes or until golden.

Whip the cream and whip in a little sugar.

Spread a small amount between the layers and a generous amount over top.

Sprinkle remaining slivered almonds on top.

Liberace's Exceptional and Extraordinary Angel Bling Cake Pie

2 egg whites

pinch of salt

½ cup sugar

⅛ teaspoon cream of tartar

¾ cup chopped nuts

1 cup heavy cream

1 teaspoon vanilla

Serves 6

Preheat oven to 275 degrees (F).

Beat the egg whites with salt until almost stiff.

Beat in the sugar, a tablespoon at a time.

Add cream of tartar and nuts.

Spoon into a greased 9-inch pie plate and bake about an hour.

Cool.

Whip the cream, add vanilla, and spread over the pie.

Chill.

Liberace with his mouth full.

unapologetic Brown Betty

6 slices dry white bread or

    2 cups breadcrumbs

⅓ cup melted butter

2 pounds cooking apples, peeled,

    cored and thinly sliced

1 cup brown sugar

¼ teaspoon salt

½ teaspoon cinnamon

½ teaspoon nutmeg

2 tablespoons lemon juice

2 teaspoons grated lemon rind

Serves 6

Cut the bread into very small cubes or use breadcrumbs.

Toss with the melted butter and line the bottom of a shallow 1½-quart baking dish with a third of the crumb-butter mixture.

Cover with half the apples.

Mix sugar, salt, cinnamon and nutmeg.

Add a third of the crumbs and half the sugar mixture.

Sprinkle with half the lemon juice and rind.

Add the remaining apples and top with remaining ingredients.

Cover dish and bake 40 minutes.

Remove cover, increase heat to 400 degrees (F) and brown for 10 minutes.

Liberace and his mother
discuss dinner plans.

NUSSTORTE

5 eggs, separated

1 cup sugar

2 cups (8 ounces) chopped
   filberts

3 tablespoons breadcrumbs

2 tablespoons rum

red currant jelly

rum-flavored whipped cream

Serves 8

Preheat oven to 350 degrees (F).

Beat the egg yolks with sugar until fluffy.

Add the filberts, breadcrumbs and rum.

Beat egg whites to stiff peaks and carefully fold into yolk mixture.

Line two or three 8- or 10-inch cake pans with a large sheet of waxed paper that will overlap rims to make cake removal easier.

Bake torte in 2 or 3 layers about 20 minutes.

Spread the cooled layers with currant jelly and top with whipped cream flavored with rum.

Liberace was inspired to place a candelabrum on his performance pianos after viewing a movie about the life of Chopin entitled *A Song to Remember*. He felt that it would draw the audience's attention when he performed in small clubs.

FaBULOUS FLOrentines

1 cup mixed candied cherries,
with other fruit and peel

1/3 cup finely chopped almonds

1/4 cup finely chopped white
raisins

1/4 cup butter

1/4 cup sugar

1 tablespoon light corn syrup

1 teaspoon lemon juice

1/2 cup sifted flour

6 ounces semisweet chocolate,
melted

Makes about 45

Preheat oven to 350 degrees (F).

Mix the fruit, peel, almonds and raisins.

Heat the butter, sugar, corn syrup and lemon juice in a saucepan.

Toss the fruit in the flour and stir into the butter mixture.

Drop by teaspoonful onto a buttered baking sheet, leaving plenty of room in between, and flatten slightly with the bottom of a moist glass.

Bake about 10 minutes until the edges are lightly browned.

After a minute, lift each with a spatula, turn over onto a wire rack and cover the flat (top) side with the melted chocolate.

Liberace with
Sister M. Adele Meiser.

MR. SHOWMANSHIP'S FLOATING ISLAND

118

5 eggs

½ cup sugar

3 cups milk, scalded

1 teaspoon vanilla

pinch of salt

Serves 6

Separate the eggs and beat the yolks slightly with a fork and mix with 3 tablespoons of sugar.

Stir the hot milk slowly into the eggs.

Pour into the top of a double boiler over simmering hot water and cook until the mixture coats a spoon.

Add vanilla, transfer to bowl and chill.

Add salt to egg whites and beat until stiff.

Add the remaining sugar gradually while beating.

Drop mixture one tablespoon at a time into boiling water.

After 2 minutes, remove with a slotted spoon.

Place on top of the chilled custard.

At one point, Liberace owned thirty-nine full-sized pianos.

i-Love-Liberace Raspberry Sherbet

6 packages frozen unsweetened raspberries

1 cup superfine sugar

2 tablespoons lemon juice, curaçao, or Cointreau

Serves 8 to 10

Thaw the berries, sprinkle with sugar and let stand an hour. Frozen berries have more juice and are better for this recipe than fresh.

Add the lemon juice or liqueur.

Place in blender container, purée, then strain.

Freeze purée.

Taste after an hour. If it is icy, remove, thaw slightly, beat well and refreeze.

meringue kisses

1/8 teaspoon salt

3 egg whites

1 cup sugar

1/2 teaspoon vanilla

1/3 cup diced candied fruit or

    1/2 teaspoon instant coffee

or cocoa

Makes about 30

Preheat oven to 275 degrees (F).

Add salt to egg whites and beat until stiff.

Add the sugar a tablespoon at a time, beating until the sugar is dissolved and the meringue stands in stiff peaks.

Fold in the vanilla, and the fruit or coffee or cocoa.

Drop one spoonful at a time onto greased cookie sheets and bake an hour until lightly browned.

zuppa inglese

1 ten-inch round sponge cake

½ cup sweet vermouth, sweet
     sherry or Marsala wine

½ cup chopped nuts

5 seedless oranges, peeled
     and sectioned

candied orange peel, cut up

9 egg yolks

⅔ cup sugar

1 cup orange juice

1½ teaspoons unflavored gelatin

2 tablespoons water

2 cups heavy cream

bing cherries

Serves 12

Cut the cake into 3 layers and sprinkle each with a third of the liquor. Have the nuts, orange sections and orange peel ready.

Beat the egg yolks with a rotary beater and gradually add the sugar, beating after each addition.

Continue beating until light and fluffy, add the orange juice and beat until well mixed.

Pour into the top of a double boiler, making sure that the boiling water in the bottom part doesn't touch the upper pan.

Beat continuously with a rotary beater 8 or 9 minutes until the custard is thick and has doubled in bulk.

Soften the gelatin in 2 tablespoons of water, heat until dissolved and add to the custard.

Put the pan in cold water to chill.

Put the top layer of the cake onto a plate, spread a third of the cold custard on the cake, arrange a third of the orange sections on the custard and sprinkle with some nuts and a little orange peel.

Put the second layer of cake on and repeat the process with custard, orange sections, the remaining nuts and a little candied orange peel.

Put on the top layer of cake and heap the remaining custard on it. If some of the sauce between the layers is pressed out, smooth it onto the sides of the cake.

Refrigerate.

All this may be done the day before.

Before serving, whip the cream, spread some of it on the sides and pile the rest on the top of the cake.

Sprinkle the center with bits of candied orange peel.

Garnish the platter with groupings of the remaining orange sections and pitted bing cherries stuffed with candied orange peel.

BLITZ TORTE

1 cup flour

½ teaspoon baking powder

pinch of salt

½ cup butter

1²/₃ cups sugar

4 eggs: separated, plus

    1 egg white

6 tablespoons milk

1 teaspoon vanilla

1 cup walnuts, pecans, or

    slivered toasted almonds

whipped cream

nuts, chocolate curls and/or

    berries

Filling:

2 tablespoons lemon juice

½ teaspoon grated lemon rind

⅓ cup water

½ cup sugar

2 tablespoons flour

3 egg yolks, beaten

Serves 8

Preheat oven to 325 degrees (F).

Sift dry ingredients together. Cream the butter with ²/₃ cup sugar.

Beat egg yolks and add.

Add the dry ingredients alternately with milk and vanilla.

Pour into two 9-inch buttered and floured cake pans.

Make a meringue by beating the egg whites until stiff, and then beating in the remaining cup of sugar, a little at a time, beating thoroughly after each addition. The meringue must be very stiff.

Spread over both pans of cake batter and dot with 1 cup nuts.

Bake about 40 minutes.

Meanwhile, make the filling by combining all the ingredients and cook in the top of a double boiler over simmering hot water.

When mixture has thickened, remove from heat.

Cool cake and pile the filling over one meringue.

Set the other layer on top so the second meringue is on top of the cake. Or, turn it upside down with the meringues in the center. Either way, cover the top with whipped cream, and garnish with more nuts, chocolate curls and/or berries.

POLISH STUFFED DOUGHNUTS

4 cups flour

1 teaspoon salt

3 cakes warm yeast

2 cups warm milk

2/3 cup sugar

2 cups jam (or 1 pound prunes
plus 1 tablespoon sugar,
1/4 teaspoon cinnamon and
2 teaspoons lemon juice)

8 egg yolks

3 tablespoons melted butter or
oil

2 tablespoons rum

deep fat for frying

superfine sugar

Serves 12 to 20

Sift the flour and salt together.

Break the yeast into the warm milk, add 1 tablespoon sugar and 1 cup of the sifted flour. Set aside in a warm place for about ½ an hour, to double in bulk.

Beat the egg yolks with the remaining sugar until fluffy.

Add the remaining flour, butter and rum.

Add the yeast mixture and beat until smooth. Set aside again in a warm place, for about an hour, to double in bulk.

For filling, cook the prunes until soft. Drain and remove the pits. Mash and return to the pot with sugar, cinnamon and lemon juice and cook a few minutes until thick.

Cool.

Punch down the dough and make plum-sized balls.

Place on a floured board and poke a hole in the sides.

Fill with about 1 teaspoon jam or prune purée mixture. Or, roll out on the board about ¾ inch thick, cut in to pieces, place a teaspoon of jam or prune mixture on one piece and cover with another piece, pinching edges together.

Let rise again for half an hour and fry in 375-degree (F) deep fat until browned.

Turn as they fry, as they will bob to the surface.

Drain on paper towel and sprinkle with superfine sugar.

Liberace poses behind a cake presented to him by Southern Nevada Memorial Hospital.

Liberace transported audiences to a dazzling world of color, jovial music, glittering costumes and self-deprecating humor. His legend lives on in the Liberace Museum in Las Vegas, which houses his collections of rare and antique pianos, classic cars, famous sequined and bejeweled costumes, glittering stage jewelry and rare antiques, as well as his private papers and memorabilia.

Since 1976, the Liberace Museum has been the key funding arm for the Liberace Foundation for the Performing and Creative Arts. The Foundation has helped talented students pursue careers in the performing and creative arts through scholarship assistance and has awarded more than five million dollars in scholarship grants to more than one hundred universities, schools and educational organizations. Liberace Foundation scholarships are administered directly by each college.

A portion of the proceeds from this book directly benefits the Liberace Foundation.

Liberace scholars have attended:

American Academy of Dramatic Arts
American Boychoir School
American College of Musicians
Appalachian State University
Arizona State University
Arkansas Arts Center
Augustana College
Ball State University
Bard College
Bennett College
Berklee College of Music
Berry College
Bethany College
The Boston Conservatory
Brevard Music Center
Brooklyn College Conservatory
    of Music
California Institute of the Arts
California State University,
    Sacramento
California State University, Sonoma
Centenary College of Louisiana
Central Methodist College
Chapman University
Chautauqua Institution
Chicago Academy for the Arts
College of Charleston

Columbia College Chicago
Columbia University
Columbus College of Art & Design
Cornish College of the Arts
Crossroads School
    for Arts & Sciences
Curtis Institute of Music
Dixie College
East Carolina University
Eastman School of Music
Fashion Institute of Technology
Florida State University
Fordham University
Gallaudet University
Illinois State University
Indiana University
The Juilliard School
Las Vegas Music Festival
Longy School of Music
Loyola University
Manhattan School of Music
Maplehill School
Marquette University
Nevada Ballet Theatre
Nevada School of the Arts
New England Conservatory
New School University

North Carolina School of the Arts
Northern Illinois University
Northwestern University
Oberlin College
Oklahoma City University
Old Dominion University
Peabody Institute
Radford University
Rocky Mountain College
San Francisco Conservatory of Music
San Francisco Opera Center
Settlement Music School
Sherwood Conservatory of Music
Southern Nazarene University
St. Louis Symphony Music School
Third Street Music School Settlement
Towson University
University of California, Los Angeles
University of California, Irvine
University of Central Oklahoma
University of Cincinnati
    Conservatory
University of Denver
University of Idaho
University of Maine
University of Miami
University of Michigan

University of Minnesota
University of Missouri, Kansas City
University of Nevada, Las Vegas
University of North Texas
University of Notre Dame
University of South Florida
University of Southern Mississippi
University of Southwestern Louisiana
University of Texas at Austin
University of Wisconsin, Platteville
University of Wyoming
Virginia Polytechnic Institute
Viterbo University
Wayne State University
Weber State University
West Milwaukee High School
West Texas A&M University
Western Illinois University
Western Michigan University
Western State College of Colorado
Westminster College
    of Salt Lake City
Wichita Center for the Arts
Wisconsin Conservatory of Music
Yavapai College/Summer Arts
    Institute
Young Musicians Foundation

"There was no escaping Mom's cooking. Little wonder I needed three sizes of clothes."

PHOTO CREDITS

Except as noted here, photographs in *Joy of Liberace* are from the Liberace Archive of the Liberace Museum.

Photographs of Liberace and Elvis Presley, Liberace and Barbra Streisand, and the Riviera marquee are
    courtesy of the Riviera Hotel and Casino and Las Vegas News Bureau.

All food and product photographs are the work of Barrett's Photography.

Goblets and glasses are from Liberace's personal service. They were made in replica of a service he admired
    that was owned by Queen Elizabeth II. Courtesy of the Liberace Museum.

Silver serving trays are from Liberace's personal service. Courtesy of the Liberace Museum.

Silverware is from the collection of author—they belonged to Grandma and Grandpa, lifelong Liberace fans.

ABOUT THE AUTHORS

Karan Feder is an award-winning Hollywood costume designer who has designed many productions for film, television and stage. She also spends time knee-deep in rhinestones and bugle beads as part of her restoration and conservation efforts for the Liberace costume and image archives. Her signature Karan Feder handbag collection was honored with the prestigious Fresh Face Award and enjoys a global following.

Michael Feder is a lifelong entrepreneur with a background in law and business. He leads the licensing efforts for the Liberace Foundation, and is the unfeathered friend of Olive, the fine-feathered parrot, as well as author of *Olive Parrot Shares Her Birthday*. Together the Feders are the authors of *Liberace, Your Personal Fashion Consultant* and are principals in Fame Farm, which creates and executes branding strategies for celebrity clients. The couple lives in Las Vegas.